CREATIVELY REAPING THE HARVEST
Using the Tea as an Outreach Ministry

By Vera LeRay Warner

Photographs by Yvonne Guiou
Bad Aibling, Germany

Copyright © 2017 by Vera LeRay Warner
All rights reserved. No part of this publication may be reproduced, stored in a retrieval system, or transmitted in any form or by any means without prior permission of the publisher.

Scriptures taken from the HOLY BIBLE, NEW INTERNATIONAL VERSION ® Copyright © 1973, 1978, 1984 by International Bible Society. Used by permission of Zondervan Publishing House. All rights reserved.

The "NIV" and "New International Version" trademarks are registered in the United States Patent and Trademark Office by the International Bible Society. Use of either trademark requires the permission of the International Bible Society.

ISBN: 978-0-9713072-0-9

Published by:

In His Image Publishing
P.O. Box 236552
Cocoa, FL 32923

CONTENTS

Dedication	i
Acknowledgments	ii
Introduction	iii
Chapter One. Tea for Two: Intimacy with Christ	1
Chapter Two. Fill Me Up and Pour Me Out	12
Chapter Three. Dressed for the Occasion	21
Chapter Four. My Name Is…I'm a Daughter of the King	32
Chapter Five. The Invitation	42
Chapter Six. The Woman in the Mirror	49
Chapter Seven. Precious Moments	58
Chapter Eight. The Bride of Christ	65
Prayer of Commitment	72
Prayer of Re-Commitment	73

DEDICATION

Geraldine Virginia Smith Yearling

You are one of the most creative women whom I am privileged to know. You are the one who first inspired me to write. Thank you for giving me life and for all the years of encouragement. We truly can rise above the circumstances. I love you Ma.

ACKNOWLEDGMENTS

I am deeply indebted to three women who took the time to contribute to the completion of this project.

Jacqueline Hawkins, a gifted intercessor and a poet graciously contributed "Daughter of Zion." I thank you my dear sister and my forever friend (now deceased).

Patty Moore, Ministry to the Military, Church of God Cleveland, Tennessee who's editing of several chapters was a godsend. Your words of encouragement compelled me to see this book through to completion.

Brenda Gunter, Church of God Cleveland, Tennessee International Women's Ministries Board. You went above and beyond in lending a hand to edit and offer suggestions. Your contribution to the work gave it a "touch of class." What an elegant lady you are (now deceased).

To all my wonderful tea partners; Willie and Carolyn Courtney, Stephanie Gant, Linda Hickey, Marilyn Joyce, Tracey Mixon, Diana Nicoson, Danis Patton and Sharon Cole. Keep the pot warm guys!

To my life partner – my husband and my best friend, Michael, who has been so patient and so and through the many nights that I sat up late at the computer. I love you honey!

Finally, but not at all least or last, is the glory that I give to my heavenly Father. Lord, you have once again proved to me that you are still the creator of the universe and that it is from you that innovative, productive and progressive ideas come to us for the building up of your kingdom. Thank you for speaking to my heart.

INTRODUCTION

In 1990, the Lord spoke to my heart and He said, "You will minister to many women." My immediate response to my Lord was, "Surely you jest Lord." But soon I found myself living in Augsburg, Germany and within a few months I was elected President of my church's Women's Ministry, as well as President of the Protestant Women of the Chapel. God says what He means and means what He says.

My first invitation to speak to a group of women while in Europe was in Olney, England. It was there that I fell in love with the custom of the tea. My excitement led me to seek the Lord as to how this beautiful custom could be used as a tool for the building up of His kingdom. It was during this time spent with my Lord that I discovered, for myself, just how He can take natural things and teach us great spiritual truths. The ideas began to flow and soon the beautiful custom of the tea became an annual event in our church that was used as a ministry tool for outreach.

The writing of this book was birthed from a simple word from the Lord, "You will minister to many women." The ideas suggested are a culmination of the many teas hosted in both the United States and Europe, and in churches of many different denominations. The results have always been the same; the Lord was glorified, in that hearts were touched and lives were forever changed. May the ideas contained in this book serve as a catapult for your own inspiration and creativity.

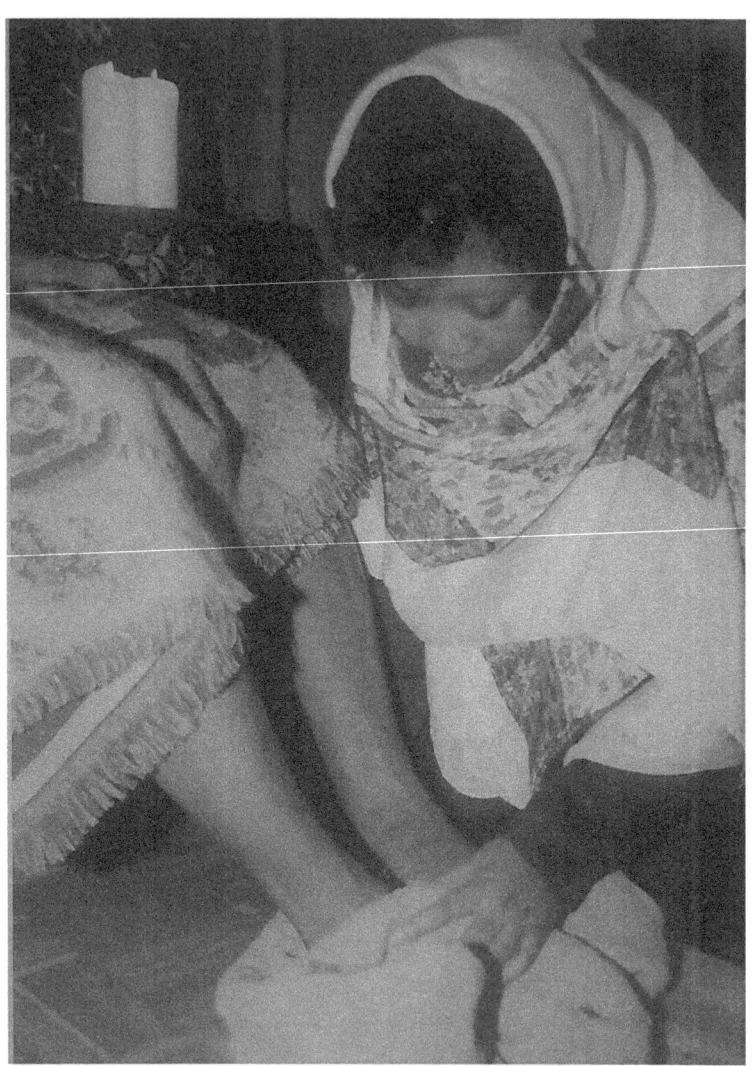

CHAPTER ONE
Tea for Two: Intimacy with Christ

Two are better than one, because they have a good return for their work: if one falls down, his friend can help him up. But pity the man who fails and has no one to help him up! Also, if two lie down together, they will keep warm. But how can one keep warm alone? Though one may be overpowered, two can defend themselves. A Cord of three strands is not quickly broken. (Ecclesiastes 4: 9-12)

Many years ago, my mentor, Helen McDowell, gave me a very beautiful miniature plate as a gift. On this plate is pictured two little girls, all dressed up, sitting at a beautifully set table and they are having tea. The inscription on the plate includes two key words, "cares and shares." I have since learned that caring and sharing is the very essence of any productive relationship.

The living breathing word of God is an expression of relationship from beginning to end. It is an expression of God's relationship with us as well as what our relationships should be with one another.

In the beginning, God Created Adam and said, "it is not good that man should be alone." He then created or fashioned a companion suitable for His man. She was called Eve, his helpmate, someone he could love and build a relationship with. She was someone whom he could give to and receive from, someone to talk with and listen to, laugh with and grow with. God had given him someone who had been created especially for him. Oh, how God must have loved Adam and in turn Adam loved God and through God, Adam also loved Eve.

Two are better than one, because they have a good return for their work...

The days were evil and full of wickedness and violence and it grieved the heart of God so much that He regretted having created man. The relationship, at this time, between God and man was not at all what it should have been. The relationship had long since ceased to be what God had initially intended. Man had allowed himself to become corrupt. But there was a man named Noah who, in the midst of it all, found favor in the eyes of the Lord. Noah had a love relationship with his God. The Lord trusted Noah and began to reveal His plan to bring judgment upon His creation. Even in God's judgment we see his love and mercy come radiating through as Noah, his wife, their sons and their son's wives were spared. The Lord also chose every kind of animal, one male and one female of its kind to once again pro-create – repopulate the earth. It took two to create another of its kind; neither male nor female of the species could do it alone.

Two are better than one, because they have a good return for their work...

I read the account of Naomi and Ruth, a mother and daughter-in-law whose relationship was built upon love and because it was based on love it produced loyalty. These two women who had found themselves left alone by the deaths of the men they loved, suddenly found their lives joined together, more than ever now, through adversity. These circumstances would ultimately serve as the vehicle God would use to bring about His purpose for their lives.

> *Two are better than one, because they have a good return for their work: if one falls down, his friend can help him up. But how can one keep warm alone?*

I further read the account of Mary and Martha, the sisters of Lazarus. I see how different they were in personality. Martha, probably the eldest, I imagine was a wonderful organizer, a servant who loved the Lord and was eager to attend to His every need. She may have been an anxious sort of woman, probably, a perfectionist. Then there was Mary, her sister, who also loved the Lord and chose not to be bothered or encumbered with the household chores, but rather chose to sit at the Lord's feet. The Lord himself said of her..." but one thing is needed, Mary has chosen what is better, and it will not be taken away from her." She sat at the feet of her Lord, hanging onto His every word, truly a love relationship between the Master and His servant, and the Teacher and His pupil, but more than that – a sinner and her Savior.

I am thoroughly convinced that the Lord is more concerned about our relationship with him than the work we do for him. It is out of our relationship with him that our works are birthed. To attempt to work for him without relationship with him would only produce substandard striving. It is in working with the Lord the fruitful service is produced.

Two are better than one, because they have a good return for their work: if one falls down, his friend can help him up. But how can one keep warm alone?

Have you ever imagined what it would be like to have the Lord come to tea? You might start off by sending him an invitation indicating the date, time and place and including the RSVP. The one thing that you could count on is that no matter the day, time or place, the Lord is never too busy to accept the invitation. He never has to check his calendar; his RSVP is yes, yes, yes! Yes, to the day, yes to the time and yes to the place. We serve a God who can be reached 24 hours a day, 7 days a week.

In preparation for this tea you may think, "Oh, the King of Glory is really coming." So, you set about cleaning the entire house from top to bottom. You absolutely must set out your best and once everything is set, you decide that your best is not good enough. But, is all this necessary? Didn't the Lord tell his disciples, *"You are my friends if you do what I command. I no longer call you servants, because a servant does not know his master's business. Instead I have called you friends, for everything that I learned from my father I have made known to you."* The Lord is letting us know that He has taken us into his confidence – there is to be an intimate relationship – we are His friends.

We are free to be ourselves with our closest friends. We don't have to try and impress them. They accept us just as we are. Neither must we try and impress the Lord. He knows everything about us and loves us unconditionally. In fact, He knows us better than we even know ourselves. Oh, what freedom to know that we can be ourselves with him!

Our relationship with the Lord is to be one of loving and caring and sharing. We love Him only because He first loved us. We can share with others who He is because He has revealed himself to us.

The Lord desires to develop that love relationship with each one of us. He desires to spend time with us so that He may lavish his love upon us. He desires to reveal his ways to us. It is when we sit at the feet of the Lord – spending quiet time with him that we truly get to know him and get to know ourselves.

I encourage you to live in continual fellowship with the Lord. Become determined to grow in such intimacy with him, that even if He whispers, you will hear and instantly obey.

Remember… "though one may be overpowered, two can defend themselves. A cord of three strands is not quickly broken.

We are in covenant with Almighty God!

LET'S GET CREATIVE

By using the theme "Tea for Two", the main spiritual focus would be how our relationship with Christ is the single most important thing in life. The secondary focus would be our relationship with one another. This would be a wonderful opportunity for each lady to invite another lady who does not know the Lord. Remember that the goal is reaping the harvest by sharing the love of God.

It is always best to send out the invitations at least two weeks in advance. You could use store bought or you may want to design your own, in keeping with your theme. An example for the wording could be:

> Daughters of the King
> Cordially invite you to
> afternoon tea.
> Saturday, June 10th at 3:00 PM
> RSVP

Remember RSVP stands for "repondez s'il vous plait" and means, in French, "please let me know if you can come."

This theme is ideal for a smaller group, but can be used for a larger group as well. If you have a smaller group, you could set up small tables and seat only two ladies per table. You could put a tea service on each table, thus making it more intimate and giving the opportunity for one on one service as well as ministry.

You may want to include songs in your program that would point to Christ. Some examples are; "Rose of

Sharon, Daystar, Jesus Is the Sweetest Name I Know or I Keep Falling in Love with Him." You could also have one of the ladies perform a short skit, for example, "A Love Letter to Jesus." The only props that you would need for this skit would be a table, chair, Bible, pen and paper.

Your food should be kept simple. You may want to prepare finger sandwiches, cookies, anything that is bite sized and that does not ooze or drip would be appropriate. And of course, you would have tea and or lemonade if you choose.

VERA LERAY WARNER

A LOVE LETTER TO JESUS

(Lady is sitting at small table with Bible, pen, and paper. She has pen in hand and looks as if she's thinking, intensely, about what to write. She starts to both write and speak.)

Dear Lord:

I think about how my life used to be before coming to know you, and my emotions seem so contradictory. On the one hand, I regret that I waited so long to serve you – of all that wasted time. I think of the times that I knew you were wooing me with your love and I resisted and ran from the nudging in my heart. On the other hand, I am overjoyed that you didn't give up on me. You continued to draw me and one day I just stopped running from you and I ran into your open arms.

You accepted me just as I was and you forgave me and cleansed me and filled my heart and now I love you more than life itself. Thank you Lord for saving me. Thank you for loving me unconditionally.

Lord, I brought a friend with me today. She is just like I was. She feels empty inside and she doesn't realize that you are the one – the only one who can fill that void. Lord, please help my friend. I love her so much Lord and I know you love her more. Surround her with people who will demonstrate your love to her. And especially help me to truly love her with your love and show her that I love her. Help me to help her see that you offer her eternal life. Open her eyes Lord and remove the veil from her heart. Extend your hand of mercy and grace and embrace her with your love. I love you Lord and I thank you for my life. Please be merciful to my friend.

Your child,

_____

At this point you may want to play the song or have someone sing, "Can You Reach My Friend."

VERA LERAY WARNER

CHRIST AND ME, ME AND CHRIST

You stood at the door and knocked
And I chose to let you in.
No longer am I an outsider
I am now your friend.

Oh, the peace that filled my soul
When you came into my heart.
Not even death itself
Can now keep us apart.

I long to know you Lord
Reveal yourself to me.
I didn't know how blind I was
Until I began to see.

To see you in your glory
To live for you each day.
To hear you when you call my name
To obey whatever, you say.

You've taken me into your confidence
I really, really belong.
You do, I do, you say, I say
You've given me a new song.

—VLW

CHAPTER TWO
Fill Me Up and Pour Me Out

But the fruit of the Spirit is love, joy, peace, patience, kindness, goodness, faithfulness, gentleness and self-control. Against such things there is no law. (Galatians 5: 22-23)

God has called us to live sanctified (set apart), holy lives. We are His called-out ones and have been sealed by His Precious Holy Spirit. We carry His inscription; therefore, we are to be vessels unto honor. We are to be vessels that have been cleansed by the blood of Jesus Christ and that have been set aside for His use.

A vessel is defined as a container used to hold something, or a person into whom some quality (as grace) is infused. The Word of God says, "…we have this treasure in earthen vessels" which refers to the indwelling of the Holy Spirit. We are indeed vessels of the Lord, fashioned by His hands, a work in progress – reaching for perfection (completeness, maturity) that comes with time as we walk in fellowship with Him.

We are to be vessels filled with the **love** of God. We are to love the Lord with all our heart, our soul, our mind and our strength. It is being filled with that unconditional love of Christ that forgives despite the hurt, knowing that we too may have been the cause of some else's pain.

We are to be vessels filled with the **joy** of the Lord. Joy, having a sense of wellbeing because we have been justified by Him and are now yielded to Him. It's like the flutter we feel inside when the one we love and yearn for walks into the room. It is that sweet sensation we feel when something good is about to happen. It is sweet contentment that all is well on the inside even though everything is going wrong on the outside.

We are to be vessels filled with the **peace** of God. Peace, freedom from fear that wants to make us distrust. Peace, a sense of well-being. Peace that rises from with us as we focus upon Him and refuse to be carried away by worry of frustration. Peace, taking our concerns to the Lord while at the same time thanking Him for what He has already done for us, what He is presently doing and what He will do for us in the future.

We are to be vessels filled with **patience**. Patience, the endurance of opposition, which helps us to be slow to anger, and not quick tempered. We patiently put up with the shortcomings of others. Patience is hanging on and trusting, enduring the hardship of life, yet living victoriously at the same time.

We are to be vessels filled with **kindness**. Kindness is love being manifested in our actions. We are to be kindhearted to one another. It is not just what we say to one another, but also how we say it. It is helpfulness to others that can only be a result of the personal experience of God's grace.

We are to be vessels filled with **goodness**. Goodness is the deliberate preference of right over wrong. You make a choice to follow what is good and right. It is living a life that is morally upright and pleasing to the Lord, knowing that apart from God our goodness would never be good enough.

We are to be vessels filled with **faithfulness**. To be faithful is to be steadfast, dedicated, dependable, and worthy of trust. God is faithful and can be trusted to be who He says He is and to do what He says He will. We have His character; therefore, we can be steadfast, not wishy-washy and thoroughly grounded. The kind of follower, whom the Lord can say, "I trust her."

We are to be vessels filled with **humility**. Humility is total dependence upon God and respect for other people. Humility is power under control. It is allowing others to shine and at times taking the back seat. Humility leads to wisdom, takes advice and is an exalter in due time. Oh, God that you would increase in our lives and that we would decrease.

We are to be vessels filled with **temperance**. Temperance is the ability to control yourself. It is leading a disciplined life. We do all things in moderation and we are not excessive in any area. We lead well-balanced lives. We follow Christ's example and not that of the world. As we mature we are more apt to demonstrate the ability to hold our tongues, and only the law of wisdom and kindness comes forth. We have mastered our personal desires and passions and only desire the will of the Father.

My prayer is that we would truly strive to become all that God wants us to be. Vessels so filled with His presence and His power that we indeed overflow and pour out to others.

LET'S GET CREATIVE

The workable focus is being a vessel that God can use in our service to Him. The teapot becomes that thing in the natural that conveys a spiritual truth.

This theme would be perfect to use for a Mother/Daughter Banquet. You could involve all age groups. The younger girls could dress up in their mothers' dresses, hats, shoes, jewelry etc. and perform, "I'm A Little Teapot", the teenage girls could dress up as tea bags and model period costumes. As they are modeling they would describe the many several types of teas and how they are best served. You could call this segment of the program "Pots on Parade."

Once again you could have your music compatible with your theme. Fill My Cup, Lord is one of my favorites and if used at the end of the program would be very effective in driving the theme home.

It would be an excellent idea to use teapots filled with fresh flowers, as your centerpieces. You might even be able to find miniature teapots to give away as favors. It might also be a clever idea to go a bit more formal with this theme. It would be nice if you would use china and linen tablecloths and napkins. You might also use place cards and put a favor at each setting. I would suggest having a separate beverage table. Offer several types of teas for tasting and label each one. Make sure that you make available the appropriate sweetener (either lump sugar or honey) and include lemon slices and cloves, if you prefer. It would also be nice to offer punch or lemonade for the non-tea drinkers.

Your food may consist of teacakes, petit fours, finger sandwiches, chocolate dipped strawberries, several types of cookies and the list goes on. Just remember that presentation is everything!

Bon Appetit!

"POTS ON PARADE"

Miss Assam: Assam is an Indian tea. It is a full-bodied tea and is refreshing to drink on a sweltering day. It is most favored at breakfast or mid-morning.

Miss Ceylon: Ceylon is grown in Sri Lanka and there are four types of this tea. It is usually golden, in color, and excellent as a mid-morning drink. It has a delicate taste and is best when served with lemon and ice.

Miss Chamomile: Chamomile is an herbal tea. If you have respiratory problems or abdominal discomfort, try this tea with honey.

Miss Kenyan: Kenyan is an important ingredient in blended teas, but is also a specialty tea. It is a full-bodied coppery colored beverage. It is great to have as the first drink of the day.

Miss Darjeeling: Darjeeling is also an Indian tea, grown in the foothills of the Himalayas. It is known as the champagne" of teas. It is wonderful as a breakfast tea.

Miss Earl Grey: Earl Grey is categorized as a special blend. It is one of the best-known specialty teas and is a combination of black China and Darjeeling teas with a touch of bergamot. It can be served hot or with ice, but is best with cream and sugar. It is a favorite afternoon tea.

VERA LERAY WARNER

FILL ME UP AND POUR ME OUT

Fill me with your love Lord
A love so kind and true
Love that always forgives
Is the love that I pursue.

Fill me with your joy Lord
Make my heart to sing,
Here I stand before you Lord
To you my heart I bring.

Fill me with your peace Lord
Take away the fear,
Flood my mind with calmness
I want to clearly hear.

Fill me with patience Lord
Enduring and steadfast,
Looking ahead to the future
Letting go of my past.

Fill me with kindness Lord
Help me help the poor,
Truly make my heart Lord
A great big open door.

Fill me with goodness Lord
Following what is good,
Living day by day
As only you say I should.

Fill me with faithfulness Lord
I want to be trusted by you,

CREATIVELY REAPING THE HARVEST

Trusted to obey your word
To do what you ask me to.

Fill me with humility Lord
No pride in me to find,
Change my heart, My Lord, My God,
Please renew my mind.

Fill me with humility Lord
Self-control is the way,
To get the best out of life
Each and every day.

And when I am filled to overflowing
pouring out to others love, joy, peace,
patience, kindness, goodness, faithfulness,
humility and temperance,

I will be reflecting the image of your Christ.
Amen
Amen
Amen

—VLW

CHAPTER THREE
Dressed for the Occasion

Therefore, as God's chosen people, holy and dearly loved, clothe yourselves with compassion, kindness, humility, gentleness and patience. (Colossians 3:12)

The Victorian Era was one of the most interesting times in history. Some considered it as the "Age of Innocence." It was a time when modesty was the custom of the day and good breeding meant good manners. It was a time when much attention was paid to the way a young lady dressed and elaborate was the norm. Young women would spend hours preparing for afternoon tea or the ball that she had been waiting months to attend. The ball was such an important event that neither a regular dress nor last year's dress would do. A lot of time was spent on choosing just the right material. The color of it most certainly should complement one's complexion and somewhat match the color of the eyes, thus making one even more alluring.

The word of God has something to say about clothing, but more about being clothed. We are admonished to be clothed with compassion, kindness, humility, gentleness and patience. I believe that the Lord is more concerned with how we are clothed on the inside than our outward appearance. Yet, when we allow the Holy Spirit to groom us internally, the effect can even be a more beautiful exterior.

The women in Paul's day were encouraged not to let their focus be upon the outward, but on the meek and quiet spirit, which was and is of immense value. There is nothing more beautiful than a woman who loves and who serves the Lord with all that she has within her. The Scriptures are saying the same thing to us today. We must allow the Lord to so such a work within us that our lives would truly reflect being hidden behind the cross, and when we are looked upon, when our lives are examined, the first thing to be noticed will be Christ in us, the hope of glory. We will have the love of God within our hearts and everything we do will be motivated by His love. We will have a burden for the lost, weeping many tears over the sin, despising the sin, but loving the sinner. We will be kind hearted and there will be evident in our lives, gentleness, but also strength that could only come from the indwelling of the Spirit of God. We will come to really, really know that without Him we would be nothing and can do nothing apart from God.

Oh, we are to be clothed with the glory of God as before the fall! Christ has made a way for us to regain our innocence before the Father. We are in the world but we are not of the world. We are to crucify the flesh, daily, so that we are truly controlled by the Spirit of God. The norm for us is to walk in obedience and never should second- guess the Lord. We will hear Him when He speaks and instantly obey. If we are to come to this place in our relationship with the Lord, we must allow Him to change us from the inside out. This is to be done no matter what it might cost us.

Our daily prayer should be; Lord, I stand before you a model made of clay. I am asking you to break me, mold me, dress me – clothe me with your garments that I may be the salt and the light, that living epistle and an ambassador for your kingdom. Amen

LET'S GET CREATIVE

This theme would be wonderful for introducing the ladies to the customs and courtesies of the "Victorian Era." The invitations should be very formal. You may even want to have someone write them, by hand, in calligraphy. This would be the perfect setting to use place cards and to even have a silver tray at the entrance for each lady to leave her calling card. You may include a calling call for each lady, in the invitation as a courtesy to your guest.

Example Invitation:

> *In His Image: Women of*
> *Excellence Ministries*
>
> *Requests the pleasure*
> *of your company for High Tea.*
>
> *Saturday, February 16th*
> *Five o'clock PM*
>
> *777 Glory Road*
> *R.S.V.P.*
> *555-7777*

Example of Calling Card:

> *Lady*
> *Nicolle Michelle Holland*

When presenting the actual program, you could have several different ladies participate in giving a brief history of the Victorian Era, proper tea etiquette, the lan-

CREATIVELY REAPING THE HARVEST

guage of the flowers, gems, fan and calling card as well as a fashion show of costumes from that era. You may even want to include on your invitation that hats and gloves are welcomed, but not required.

The playing of classical music as the women are coming in would be an excellent touch and you might even consider having someone play the violin or a simple CD would do just fine.

As this is a very formal tea you may want to be quite elaborate as far as the food is concerned. Finger Sandwiches, including opened face ones, chocolate covered strawberries, cookies dipped in chocolate, scones with Devonshire Cream, petit fours, rolled cookies, miniature quiche, miniature fruit kabobs, hot tea with lump sugar, cream, honey and lemon. Iced Tea punch or fresh squeezed lemonade. You may also want to have cakes of various kinds. Use your imagination and remember that presentation is everything! If it looks good people will usually eat it!

This would be the perfect time to use fine linen tablecloths and linen napkins. Fresh flowers, silver tea service, and china would be appropriate. Try not to use anything disposable. Candlelight would also be a welcomed touch. It would be a nice additive if you had three tiered plates and silver platters as well.

You could also have the ladies bring their own favorite teacup and saucer and have several of them tell why it is their favorite.

Make this evening extremely special!

INTERESTING VICTORIAN TIDBITS FOR YOUR TEA:

Language of the Fan:

A young lady would flirt with her fan, particularly at a ball. Each position had a significance of its own.

Fan fast – I am independent and available

Fan slowly – I am engaged

Fan with right hand in front of face – An invitation to come over

Fan with left hand in front of the face – You may leave me now

Fan opens and shut – Kiss me

Fan wide open – Love

Fan completely shut – Hate

Fan swinging on the wrist – You can see me home

Language of the Flowers:

Victorian ladies were seen during their afternoon walks carrying small bunches of flowers. From time to time they could be seen holding them up to their noses to inhale the pleasing aroma. These small bouquets were made up of very fragrant flowers, as well as herbs and became known as "nose gays" or "tussie mussies." Their purpose was to help tolerate the unpleasant odors associated with poor sanitation. But, flowers were also used to convey messages, and floral communication was an art form.

The rose, the most fragrant of flowers, along with the red tulip, represented true love and said, "I love you." The pansy said, "think of me", the violet – "the feeling is mutual." The jonquil – "say you love me too." The hibiscus meant "aflame with desire", the azalea meant a promise of high romance, and the carnation was the symbol of patience.

Language of the Gems:

The Victorians felt that gems, too, spoke a secret language of the heart. Diamonds, the hardest of stones, represented everlasting strength, eternity, and passionate love. Emeralds represented lasting affection and fidelity, sapphires – truth and faithfulness, aquamarine – courage and intelligence, amethyst – honorable intention, rubies and garnets – true love and warm affection, and pearls – gentle wisdom and modesty.

Language of the Calling Card:

At three o'clock on any given afternoon toward the end of the nineteenth century, a Victorian lady might be found pausing at the mirror, to adjust her hat as she heads out to fulfill her social duty of the day, the ceremony of paying calls.

To pay a "proper call" was a visit lasting no less than fifteen minutes and no more than thirty minutes. She kept on her hat and gloves and proceeded to make polite small talk and then left. But before leaving she would leave her calling card in the card receiver that was prominently displayed by the door. If the hostess happened not to be at home, the card would indicate the nature of her visit....

Folded upper right hand corner- she had come in person

Folded upper left hand corner – congratulations

Folded lower right hand corner – good bye

Folder lower left-hand corner – condolences

Folded entire left end of the card – she had come to visit all the women of the family

Tea Time:

Remove your gloves to eat, sip – don't slurp, napkins on your laps, sit up straight, pinkies in and bring your saucers up with your cup.

A MODEL FOR JESUS

Here I stand before you Lord
A model made of clay,
Don't know much, can't do much
You must teach me what to say.

Fashion me and shape me
Turn me inside out,
Teach me what this life of mine
Is really all about.

Give me your eyes to see with
Make my vision clear,
Fill my mouth with good things
Fill my heart with cheer.

My hands I stretch toward heaven
I want to serve with all my might,
Teach my hands to war Lord
In the Spirit, I will fight.

You've given me your armor
You've dressed me head to toe,
Through your blood, Jesus
I can defeat the foe.

I have your helmet upon my head
To protect my mind,
The breastplate of righteousness
Around my heart to bind.
Your belt of truth around my waist
To hold my weapons in place,

Your Gospel shoes upon my feet
They help me keep up the pace.

Your shield of faith within my hand
To quench every fiery dart,
Your sword of the Spirit I do wield
In the battle from the start.

Thank you Lord
You've given your best
And I am dressed and ready to do,
And now my cry to the entire world:
"Let the redeemed of the Lord say so!"

—VLW

CHAPTER FOUR
My Name is...
I'm a Daughter of the King

A good name is more desirable than great riches; to be esteemed is better than silver or gold. (Proverbs 22: 1)

As I think back over the years, it has occurred to me that society has placed much emphasis on the reputation of a person, based in part; according into which family they were born. I remember as a young person in junior high school, our principal had two children. It was because of who their father was and the reputation that he had, that there were certain things expected of them. Their father was a highly-respected man in the community, a man of integrity, and an educated man. It was because of his success in life that the children were expected to be no less than their father and were afforded many opportunities that others were not afforded.

On the other hand, there were many families who only had one parent in the home. Quite a few of these families were living at or below poverty level, and had to go on welfare. This placed a stigma on those children, and they too gained a reputation because of the family into which they happened to be born.

When you hear the name Rockefeller, the first thought that might enter your mind is wealth, and the second thought might be politics. When you hear the name

Kennedy, you might possibly think of politics, especially the presidency, or wealth, power and privilege. A child of either the Rockefeller's or Kennedy's would have certain privileges and advantages just because of the family into which they were born.

The word of God tells us that there is a Name that is above all other names – the Name of Jesus Christ. When we are saved (born again), no matter who our earthly father was or the reputation he had, we are now a part of the family of God, and He is our Father. We become daughters of the King! It is He who places a robe on our back, a ring on our finger, and shoes on our feet, announcing to the world that we are His! Just think about it. Our heavenly Father is the Creator of the universe; the One Who spoke this world into existence. Our Father is the One Who loved us so very much that He sent His Son Jesus to die a horrendous death for us, only to be risen on the third day that we would have eternal life.

We call our Father, Abba, and He affectionately calls us daughter. He has made us to be joint heirs to Jesus Christ. We are the Bride of Christ, and He has given to us His Precious Holy Spirit that we might live an overcoming life. We are indeed His daughters with all the rights and privileges that go with it. We have the privilege of serving Him for the rest of our lives and the right to claim His many promises.

Many of us do not come from socialite families. Many of us are just plain, common folk. Some may have come from backgrounds too shoddy to even speak of, yet God, in His mercy and grace, reached down to where we were and embraced us. He is continually fashioning us into what He intends for us to be. Our Father has the highest reputation, and to be renamed by Him is worthy of the highest praise!

He is saying to you and me; you are no longer lost; your name is loved! You are no longer heathen; your name is now holy! You are no longer prideful; your name is now precious! You are no longer resentful; your name is now redeemed!

If the King of Glory gives you a new name, then that name is more desirable than all the riches the world affords you. He is the one who has esteemed us by calling us His own. Thank you Father that we are "Daughters of the King."

CREATIVELY REAPING THE HARVEST

LET'S GET CREATIVE

What a wonderful theme: My Name is…I'm a Daughter of the King. This theme can be used to introduce or reacquaint us with the women on the Bible whose lives were influenced in marvelous ways by the Lord.

You could do a skit that could involve as many or as few characters as you choose. Each lady would dress up in biblical attire, and do a short narrative on various women from the Bible or she could do her own testimony. If she did a woman of the Bible, she would not reveal her name until the end of the narrative. She would close the narrative with, "My name is_____, and I am a Daughter of the King.

Using this theme could possibly minister, in a mighty way, to women who are having a problem with their identity in Christ. You could also print birth certificates listing the Lord as her heavenly Father.

You could also use the theme, "A Galilean Breakfast Tea." You could use as a color scheme; earth tones, such as beige, green, black, brown, etc. Your food could be the basic foods they had in Biblical times - fruits, nuts, breads, yogurt, boiled eggs, juice, etc. You might possibly use palm branches at each place setting to go under the plates, using some type of earthenware. In the middle of the table you could place rocks, stones along with the various names of women from the Bible on cards.

Listed below are some names of women from the Bible that would make for good narratives:

Lydia
Ruth
Deborah
Naomi
Michal
Martha
Esther
Dorcas
Woman at the Well
Mary Magdalene

DAUGHTER OF KING NARRATIVE

Oh, it is such a sweltering day out, but I must go and draw water. I am getting so weary of the stares and the gossip. This is my life and I can do what I want! So, what if I've had more than my share of husbands, is it so wrong to just want to be loved by the right man? And if he's out there I am determined to find him.

Oh, he must be a stranger in town. I've never seen him before. He looks tired and lonely sitting by the well. Oh no, he is a Jew and he has the nerve to ask me for a drink of water. "Don't you know sir that I am a Samaritan how is it that you can ask me for a drink? You know that we are to have nothing to do with one another. And besides that, you have nothing to draw with and the well is deep. You speak of this living water where can you get it? Are you greater than our father Jacob, who gave us the well and drank from it himself, as did also his sons and his flocks and herds? Sir you say that if I drink of your water that I will never thirst and that it will become in me a spring of water welling up into everlasting life? Sir, give me this water so that I won't get thirsty and have to keep coming here to draw water."

Now why is he asking me about my husband? Sir, I have no husband, but you knew that didn't you. I can see that you are a prophet. Maybe if I change the subject he will leave my personal business out of this! Our fathers worshipped on this mountain, but you Jews claim that the place where we must worship is in Jerusalem. Sir, you say that salvation is of the Jews. I know that Messiah is coming. When he comes, he will explain everything to us. You, are he? – You, are he?

Yes, it is you, you are the Messiah – my Lord and my King! Come, see a man who told me everything I ever did. Could this be the Christ? My name is never ever mentioned and yet I am a daughter of the King! I am the Samaritan Woman at the Well.

DAUGHTER OF ZION

Daughter of Zion
Lift up your eyes and see
Behold our King
Clothed in honor and majesty.

He sits upon a throne made of pure gold,
A most wonderful sight to behold.
Angels gather around and sing
Holy, holy, holy is our King.
He is the Lamb that was for sinner's slain,
And Jesus is His Precious Name.

Lift up your eyes daughter of Zion and see
The one who gives us hope and victory.
He broke the yoke of bondage and set the captives free.
All this was done on the Cross at Calvary.

He shed His blood for you and me
Bow down, worship, clap your hands and sing.
For great and awesome is His Name
The Blessed One who is forever the same.

Daughter of Zion, grab hold of the truth,
Be wise and strong and nurture our youth.
For they are the men and women of the tomorrow
In a world that is full of pain and sorrow.

Let them grow in the word of God
For there are many paths that their feet must trod.
If their souls are anchored in the Lord,
They will go abroad and spread His word.

VERA LERAY WARNER

Daughter of Zion, behold and see
The young and the old in liberty.
The battle's been won; there's the victor's crown
The army of the Lord still marches on.

Until that final day, you'll hear
The trumpet bursting through the air,
Announcing the entrance of our King,
And with the heavenly host you'll sing
Praise be to Thee who reigns in majesty.
You're a woman of beauty
A woman of grace
A woman of God
With a smiling face.

You're a mother of love
Sent from God above
With wisdom, compassion, tender, yet strong
Your family knows to whom you belong.

You're a daughter of prayer
With knees always bent
You are the one whom God has sent.
A virtuous woman you are by far
Keep shining like the "Bright Morning Star."

—Jacqueline Hawkins (Used by written permission)

CHAPTER FIVE
The Invitation

"Ho, everyone that thirsteth, come ye to the waters, and he that hath no money; come ye, buy, and eat; yea, come, buy wine and milk without money and without price. Wherefore do ye spend money for that which is not bread? And you labor for that which satisfieth not? Hearken diligently unto me, and eat ye that which is good, and let your soul delight itself in fatness." (Isaiah 55: 1- 2)

The writer starts Isaiah 55 with "Ho", a cry that goes out to the people meaning to wait, listen, take notice – be still and hear the message. It reminds me of other places in the Word where it is stated, "to *hear what the Spirit of the Lord is saying.*" As I allow my mind to reflect upon this, I can imagine a town crier of old. At night, he would go through the streets of the town with a lantern in his hand shouting "hear ye, hear ye." In other words, "*he who has an ear to hear let him hear.*"

We find here that an invitation is being extended – a simple "come." If a host were giving a party, you would know that you were invited, because you would receive an invitation. If you heard about the party and received no invitation, you might just feel left out, offended or even rejected. You could possibly even wonder, "well what's wrong with me, why wasn't I invited?" Isaiah's invitation is being extended to all – everyone is welcome to come.

The Lord says to *come to the waters*." In the day in which Isaiah lived, the people understood that to come to the waters meant the watersides, the port or the wharf. When I was a little girl my grandfather worked as a longshoreman. His job was to load and unload the ships, which came in to the port. The merchandise was usually items that had come in from other parts of the United States or other countries. This, too, was the case in Isaiah's day. The market place was right on the port or wharf. It was there that the finest of imported goods were being sold and purchased. The Lord is saying to come and see and sample the best that He has to offer.

The King of glory is inviting all who are thirsty to come. Thirst is an intense desire to partake of something. The Lord is extending an invitation to anyone who has an intense thirst within him or her. He is extending an invitation to those who are just not satisfied. He is inviting those who have no money, to come and receive, freely, that which will satisfy completely.

The Bible is full of examples of people who had no money, but who had a need. There was the woman with the issue of blood. She had spent all she had on doctors to find a cure – any cure. She needed a healing. She received her healing, and it cost her not one denarii. There was the woman at the well who took her pitcher to draw water, not realizing that she had an even deeper thirst. She received a drink of living water so that she would never have to thirst again. Then there was blind Bartemaeus, a beggar who needed to receive his sight. He received more than his natural sight. His greatest need was met in that his spiritual eyes were opened. All the aforementioned were thirsty, needy, had no money, yet they were invited to come. They were invited to come with their needs, come with no money, just come. It would make no sense to the natural mind to be told to come, buy and eat without money. To the natural mind, one could come, but surely cannot buy nourishment without money and cannot eat without food. But the gift of the grace of God is freely given, with no strings attached. How wonderful our God is to offer us His bounty without us having to pay a cent for it.

'There will be milk and wine there." The milk represents that which will nourish the soul. The wine represents that which will refresh or revive the soul. I think of Jesus at the marriage supper at Cana. They had run out of wine, and the Lord changed the plain, ordinary water into wine. The wine was of such quality that it was said that the best had been saved for last. God does all things well!

No matter what our need may be, we can always count on the Lord to forever extend an invitation to come, buy and eat. He says to *"come unto me all ye that labour and are heavy laden and I will give you rest."* God, the giver of salvation, the giver of deliverance, the giver of healing and the giver of rest is inviting you to come!

LET'S GET CREATIVE

Everyone loves a party! Without a doubt, the central idea to go along with this theme is, "The Party of All Parties." Since the theme for this tea is not exactly traditional, much care should be taken in the preparation of the invitations. Keep in mind that your target group are those who do not know Christ as their Savior and Lord.

Sample wording for invitation:

> ***In His Image: Women of Excellence Ministries***
> *requests the pleasure*
> *of your company, for*
> *afternoon tea.*
> ***Wednesday, February 16***
> ***Between three and five o'clock***
> ***R.S.V.P.***

It would be a clever idea to frame the wording with a scroll clip art, print it on parchment, roll the invitation, seal it with a wax insignia and tie it with a ribbon. This invitation is from the King of Kings!

Even though it is a tea party geared toward women, you can still give it a youthful twist. Ask each lady to bring in a photograph of herself, as a child. Number the photographs and let them try and guess the identities. You could also set up a child-sized table and chairs and set it for tea using either teddy bears or dolls. Ask several ladies to give a short testimony of how and when they accepted the invitation to become a believer. Call this part of your program, "The Little Girl Within, or "Who Do I Really Want to Be Like When I Grow Up?"

More Suggested Ideas:

Colors: Pastels

Food: Dainty Tea Sandwiches, Dainty Cookies or Pound Cake, Tea (hot and cold), or lemonade.

Decorations: Ask each lady to bring in her own place setting of china, crystal, silverware and linen napkin to use at her table. Place tea sets and doilies with an array of pastel flowers in the middle. You can also use memorabilia from each lady to continue with the decorating theme.

SIT, MY FRIEND

Sit right here, my friend
And stay a little while,
I will put the kettle on
And serve you in such style.

No fancy teapot for us
Nor linen dripping with lace,
Just a little cup of tea
Sweetened to your taste.

I may have a cookie or two
No fancy foods have I,
But I can tell you stories
That will make you cry.

Sit right here, my friend
And stay a little while,
I will put the kettle on
And serve you in such style.

—VLW

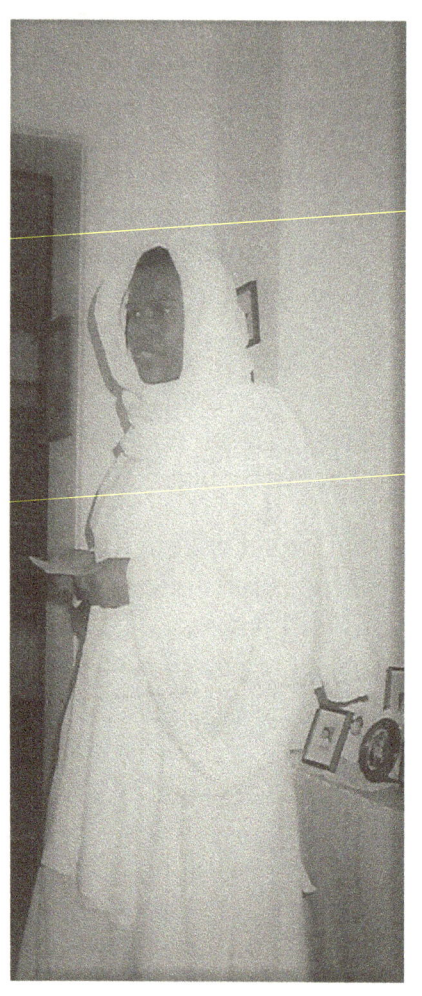

CHAPTER SIX

The Woman in the Mirror

17 Now the Lord is the Spirit; and where the Spirit of the Lord is, there is liberty. 18 But we all, with unveiled face, beholding as in a mirror the glory of the Lord, are being transformed into the same image from glory to glory, just as by the Spirit of the Lord. (2Corinthians 3: 17-18)

In chapter three of Second Corinthians the writer begins by saying that we, as children of God are living epistles. In other words, people will literally read our lives. As believers, what we do more than what we say is constantly being considered by those whom we encounter. But, we can rest in the fact that our lives have been, "written not with the ink of man" but by the Spirit of the living God. Our sufficiency is of God and not ourselves. Then the writer goes on to say that they had no need of letters of recommendation because their lives were those letters.

When my husband and I were about to leave Augusta, Georgia to go to Germany; our pastor gave us letters of recommendation. These letters were to be given to the leadership of our next church family. What fine letters they were too. But you know those words written on paper would not be worth much if our lives did not reflect what was written. The writer was telling those saints in Corinth, and it still speaks to us just as loudly today; that what their lives reflected, how they lived counted more than any words written on paper.

The Apostle Paul goes on to address the differences between the old and the new covenant. He said that the Spirit of the Lord had carved his law on their hearts instead of stone. This is the new covenant. Under the old covenant the law was engraved on tablets of stone. The old covenant represented the law and the law brought death. When Moses was given the law, his face shone with such glory that he had to cover it; but with time that brightness faded away. We have a better covenant in that the glory is no longer on the face of one man but shines on the faces of all believers who enter covenant with God. And that glory is ever increasing. The veil upon our hearts has been removed. We with unveiled faces reflect his glory. We have reflected glory that will last.

Beloved when was the last time you looked in the mirror and really looked at who was staring back? Now, I am not talking about the obvious things; two eyes-brown or blue maybe, or a nose-broad or pointed, or a mouth-full lips or thin lips with a few wrinkles thrown in or gray in your hair just beginning to appear. When was the last time you really looked at that woman in the mirror and thought about who was staring back at you? Who is that woman? Why is she on the planet? What is the Almighty's plan for her life? When will she reach her destiny? Where does God want her to go? How does she get there? Are you one of those who appear to have it altogether on the outside and on the inside, you are screaming, "Lord, I don't know who I am?" You have reasoned, "I am a believer, I go to church. I can say amen and hallelujah. I can even raise my hands on cue, yet the person inside is screaming, "Lord, I don't know who I am and sometimes I feel that I don't even know you!" If this is you; be encouraged my sister. God is still God and the work that he has begun in you - He will complete. And this is who you are:

Now, at the very moment that we were saved God instantaneously gave us a measure of his glory. Haven't you noticed how the countenance of a person changes the moment that they give their hearts to the Lord? Personally, I can go back and look at pictures of myself before I was a believer and look at myself now and I look brighter. The darkness of sin had stained my life and it took the blood of Jesus to wash it all away and to cause me to shine. Beloved we have been regenerated by the Holy Spirit and the change that has taken place in our spirits can and will be reflected on the outside. We go from glory to ever increasing glory! As we walk in obedience to the Lord; the god-life within us increases.

When Adam and Eve were created in the image of God, they were originally clothed with His glory. They reflected God's goodness, mercy, kindness, power, strength and holiness. Just imagine, mere man reflecting the glory of an Almighty God! Christ, the second Adam or the last Adam has come to restore to us that which was lost in the garden. We are to be his ambassadors-going from glory to ever increasing glory; as we allow the Spirit of God to transform our lives. We go through the process of transformation. We go through the process of being one thing and then being completely changed into something else.

It is amazing to me that we can observe creation and fins spiritual truth revealed so plainly. The butterfly, one of the most beautiful of God's creatures, did not have it's beginning with all those vibrant colors; nor was it ale to fly. The butterfly has its beginning as a rather ordinary caterpillar. To some its beginning is the most unattractive creature and certainly earth bound. For that butterfly to reach what it has been destined to be it must go through the process of metamorphosis.

The process of metamorphosis begins with the egg. We can liken this to our new birth in Jesus Christ. We are new creatures. There is no one exactly like me, "hello world here I am." At this stage, the caterpillar is very slow that it only crawls an average of about three feet per minute. As newborn believers, the spiritual growth may seem so slow at the beginning. Sometimes it seems as if we never get it together and certainly never have it altogether. Oh, how we compare ourselves to our other brothers and sister in Christ. But relax child of God, you are a work in progress and the growth may seem slow but it is steady!

The caterpillar is also very fearful as it hides from its enemies by attaching itself to the underside of leaves. I can remember when I was a babe in Christ having so many unwarranted fears, because I had not truly come to understand the authority I had been given as a child of God. As I matured in the Lord, a lot of the fears went away and were replaced with courage. So, once again, relax child of God. You are a work in progress. The caterpillar at this stage also eats non-stop. It consumes so much that in about a month's time it has outgrown its skin and burst through it several times, as its growth is continual. As we continue to feast upon the word of God, more and more of the flesh (carnality) is put to death. It becomes more and more of God and less and less of our carnal wants and desires as we are being conformed to the image of the Son.

When the caterpillar finally pops out of its last skin, it becomes a pupa. This is the short "rest stop" before it becomes an adult. It is during this period that the pupa is at total rest and the complete change from larvae to adult takes place. It has shed its last skin and makes a cocoon. The larvae will spin a mummy-like cocoon around itself, cementing it to the branch of a tree. The pupa is a Latin word which means doll and gives the impression of an infant wrapped in swaddling clothes. There was an infant born over 2,000 years ago who also was wrapped in swaddling clothes and it was because of His birth that we can experience the new birth. Inside the cocoon the pupa is completely hidden from view while its tissues are be reorganized, its structure is being broken down and its wings are developing. The pupal stage is a time of rest. We can liken this stage to the time in our walk with the Lord when our own works have ceased and we are in partnership with him. We cease to do "good things" and do good - "God things." We have learned what it means to abide in him; in his presence. We have entered such fellowship with him that even if he chooses to whisper, we hear and we obey. We find blessed contentment to just sit before him. And while in his presence we don't feel the need to speak, but we rest and listen and wait for his instructions. It is during this time of spiritual growth that the greatest changes are taking place within us. We are hidden under the shadow of his wings. He is truly our hiding place.

Right before that magnificent creature comes forth the larvae must go through tremendous struggle. That struggle is what propels it to come forth. And if the cocoon is broken by any external means the larvae will die. The struggle is necessary for God's creature to come forth at the appointed time and only God has pre-ordained what that appointed time is. It will not be a moment too soon nor a moment too late. At the appointed time the adult emerges; beautiful, mature, able to spread its wings and fly but also able to lay eggs to reproduce itself. In our walk with the Lord, beloved, know that the trials and the struggle that we experience are for our maturing. They are necessary! It is in the times of testing that we learn to trust!

Women of God, the Lord is transforming us so that we can look at that woman in the mirror and what we will see reflected will be a work in progress. We will see a woman who is in the process of being conformed to the image of the Son. Let us therefore; be determined to die to self so that we may truly live. Let us be determined to no longer be conformed to the dictates of this world, but to be transformed by the mighty hand of God as we allow him to mold us. Let us be able to say with conviction, "Change me Lord. I am the one who desires and needs to change."

LET'S GET CREATIVE

What a wonderful theme this is for an evening tea. You could start off by designing invitations in the shape of a butterfly or little hand-held mirrors. The use of framed stand-up mirrors, flowers, candle, butterflies and caterpillars on each table would be wonderful. The candlelight would bring warmth that would beautifully reflect off the mirrors.

You could give the room a garden type of setting using live flowering plants as your centerpieces. You could wrap the pots in pastel colored foil and secure the foil with coordinating wired ribbon. You could also use lots of artificial trees and plants.

Little booklets, containing the process of metamorphosis, as a reminder to the ladies of the process that we all go through would be exceptionally nice. It would also be a wonderful idea to have a couple of the ladies to do poetry readings about change. And to really make it interesting; have the poetry readings done by different generations; grandmother, daughter and granddaughter! Whatever you choose to do, glorify God and have fun!

VERA LERAY WARNER

TEATIME PREP

It's teatime again,
Put the kettle on to boil.
Let's take a little break
From our labor and toil.

Pour the heated water in
And swirl it in the pot.
We want to try and keep
Our tea nice and hot.

Finger sandwiches and scones,
A petit four or two.
Will be just the right thing
To serve along with our brew.

Jam for the scones.
Milk and sugar for the tea.
Oh, how lovely
Our teatime will be.

—VLW

CHAPTER SEVEN
Precious Moments

There is a time for everything, and a season for every activity under the heavens: a time to be born and a time to die, a time to plant and a time to uproot, a time to kill and a time to heal, a time to tear down and a time to build, a time to weep and a time to laugh, a time to mourn and a time to dance, a time to scatter stones and a time to gather them, a time to embrace and a time to refrain from embracing, a time to search and a time to give up, a time to keep and a time to throw away, a time to tear and a time to mend, a time to be silent and a time to speak, a time to love and a time to hate, a time for war and a time for peace. (Ecclesiastes 3: 1-8)

In the beginning of the word of God we are immediately introduced to time. In Genesis 1:4 we read that God said, "Let there be lights in the expanse of the sky to separate the day from the night, and then to serve as signs to mark seasons and days and years." We also read in Psalms 90:4 that a thousand years to the Lord are as a day that has just gone by. God, the originator of time does not view time in the same sense that we do. He is not limited by seconds or minutes or days. Nor is He limited by weeks or even years. Yet, in Ecclesiastes 3:1 it states that there is a time for everything, and a season for every activity under the heavens…It is further stated in verse 11 of Ecclesiastes chapter 3 that He (meaning God) hath made everything beautiful in his time…Just as God has given us seasons

CREATIVELY REAPING THE HARVEST

in the earth, I believe that there are seasons in our progressive journey of maturation in our walk of faith. Each of these seasons are, '"precious moments" in time.

First there is winter. Let's call this the season of quietly waiting upon the Lord. When I think of winter, it is quite natural for me; especially while living in Bavaria. The winters in Bavaria are known for cold winds, ice, bare trees with frozen limbs and the beauty and the stillness of fresh fallen snow. I envision snowcapped mountains and early morning stillness. I hear not a single the bird singing. It is during this season that most of my time is spend indoors as the days are relatively short and the nights are long. And because of this I am anxious for this season to end. I might even find myself a victim of "Cabin Fever." But wintertime does have its advantages. I am inside and I have pulled away from the crowds. I can sit before the Lord and allow him to rekindle his fire inside of me. I can seek him to rekindle that fire the once brought comfort, warmth, and refining has almost gone out. It has been replaced by coldness, isolation, and despondency that has slowly crept in. It is during this season that He can ignite his fire, once again, that will cause those things to thaw, thus ushering in the renewal of spring.

> *...weeping may stay for the night, but rejoicing comes in the morning. (Psalms 30: 5b)*

Before you know it, spring has arrived. We wake up to the birds singing. The flowers that were in the cold dark ground all winter have now burst out of their prisons. And inside of us, there is a stirring, a moving, an awakening; like a bear that has just come out of hibernation and is hungry! We are hungry for more of the Lord. We are hungry for those things to be birthed that were conceived during the winter season. The air is crisp and the Lord is walking with us. The Lord is restoring us and reviving us. He brings about a spiritual refreshing. Yes, spring is here; but summer is on the way!

LET'S GET CREATIVE

What a wonderful theme to focus on, "Seasons of Growth." Send out invitations that would reflect the different seasons. You could make them in the shape of a snowman for winter, a butterfly for flower for spring, a sailboat for the summer and maybe a leaf for the fall.

You could have the room where the event will be held divided into four sections; a section for each season. Here are some suggestions for the tables:

Winter: Hats, gloves, scarves, sleigh, ice skates, snowmen etc.

Spring: Flowers, butterflies, live plants, flower seeds, gardening tools, gardening gloves etc.

Summer: Sunshades, beach towel, beach ball, sand bucket, suntan lotion, beach hat, beach chairs, seashells, hammock etc.

Fall: Vegetables, foliage, bales of hay, stalks of corn, pumpkins, scare crow etc.

In planning your actual program, you could have at least one lady from each season dialogue on what it means to be in each season of life in her walk with the Lord.

The food that you serve may also reflect the seasons. Here are just a few suggestions:

Winter
Hearty sub sandwiches cut in manageable slices
Bite sized pieces of gingerbread
Hot tea served in mugs with cinnamon sticks

Spring
Dainty finger sandwiches (crust removed)
Fancy cookies of various kinds
Hot tea served using cups and saucers

Summer
Fried Chicken Drumettes
Potato Salad
Vegetable Tray
Fruit Tray
Sweet Iced Tea with Lemon

Fall
Sausage Balls
Miniature Quiche
Pumpkin and Apple Shaped Cookies
Vegetable Tray
Hot Apple Cider

THE SEASONS OF MY LIFE

Come winter come;
As I quietly sit before my Lord.
Hidden from the iciness
that would freeze my heart.
For His fire ignites my fire,
And I am warm again.

Come spring come;
As I grow in God's love.
And I bloom in His grace;
Becoming fragrant and pleasing to Him.

Come summer some;
As I labor to enter that Sabbath rest.
And reflect upon the wonder of His goodness.
All the while learning to trust;
And I am learning not to worry.

Come fall come;
As I reflect upon my Lord's goodness.
I am being changed;
powerfully, purposefully and progressively.

Come seasons of life;
For I am a canvas not yet complete.

—VLW

CHAPTER EIGHT
The Bride of Christ

I delight greatly in the Lord my soul rejoices in my God for he has clothed me with garments of salvation and arranged me in a robe of righteousness as a bridegroom adorns his head like a priest and as a bride adorned herself with her jewels. (Isaiah 61:10)

The Lord Jesus Christ took a personal interest in weddings. In fact, the first miracle he performed was at a wedding at Cana in Galilee. We read in John 2: 1-10 that Jesus his mother and his disciples were invited to be guest at a wedding. Back then weddings were elaborate celebrations that could last for a week or more. People traveled great distances, and before the actual ceremony there was usually a processional parade. The bride and her party would walk from her house and the bridegroom from the place of his choice. Their destination was the father of the groom's house. And as they went along there would be music and the scattering of flowers. Most times there would be traditional wedding songs sung; possibly even the song of *Solomon 3:6, "who is coming out of the wilderness like pillars of smoke, perfumed with myrrh and frankincense and with all the merchant's fragrant powders?"*

It was during the celebration that we find the Lord. The bride and groom may not have even fully realized that they had invited the son of God, the king of glory to their wedding. And we're about to become witnesses to his loving concern in a miraculous way. As the feasting was in full swing, the couple's joy could have easily turn into embarrassment and disappointment as they ran out of wine. But the Master in the midst told the servants to bring jars of ordinary water and he turned that ordinary water into extraordinary wine. The wine was of such exquisite quality that the master of the banquet exclaimed that, *"Everyone brings up the choice wine first and then the cheaper wine after the guests have had too much to drink, but you have saved the best till now."* The Lord does all things well. Yes, it can be safe to say that the Lord did take a special interest in weddings even though he left this earth never having been married himself. But, how wonderful it is to know that when he left he had already selected his bride and he will return for her. Take a walk with me and let us go on this romantic journey with Christ and his chosen bride.

The Selection

The Lord did not set his love on you nor choose you because you were more in number than any other people for you were the least of all peoples but because the Lord loves you and because he would keep his oath which he swore to your fathers the Lord has brought you out with a mighty hand and redeemed you from the house of bondage from the hand of Pharaoh king of Egypt. Deuteronomy 7: 7-8

The Lord is speaking to the children of Israel let them know that their deliverance did not come because of a greater number than any other nation but simply because he loved them. The Lord is saying the same thing to his church-his bride. We have been selected by God not because we have earned the right or deserved it but simply because he loves us.

The Courtship

No one can come to me unless the father who sent me draws him and I will raise him up at the last day John 6: 44

Courtship the act process or period of courting. To court means to perform actions to attract. It means to engage in social activities leading to engagement and marriage. To court means to woo and to woo means to seek or to gain, in other words, "I want you for myself and I'm coming after you. I intend to have you for my own. The Lord has chosen you and he now sets out to woo you. He does things in your life, revealing himself to you showing you his goodness to lead you to repentance. He wants you for his own. Oh, such love revealed. He makes it hard to resist!

The Proposal

"Here I am! I stand at the door and knock if anyone hears my voice and opens the door I will come in and eat with him and he with me." (Revelation 3: 20)

And finally, he comes to you and he knocks on the door of your heart. This One who has wooed you and loves you and laid down his very life for you. The one who promises to except you just as you are and to forgive you of all the wrong of your past. The one who promises you a different life and who promises to supply all your needs. The one who promises to never leave you nor forsake you. The one who promises to give you eternal life. He has finally popped the question, "Will you let me into your heart? Will you accept me as your savior and your Lord?"

The Acceptance

> *"That if you confess with your mouth, "Jesus is Lord," and believe in your heart that God raised him from the dead, you will be saved. For it is with your heart that you believe and are justified and it is with your mouth that you confess and are saved."* Romans 10: 9-10

It is at this point that you let all defenses down and with complete surrender you say, "yes." You now enter a betrothal or engagement period. It is usually at this point in the natural that the intended bride would begin making wedding plans. And one of the first things that she would do would be to choose her wedding gown. But, spiritually speaking, in our case, the bridegroom instantly gives his bride her wedding garment. It is the garment that he has purchased with his blood. The gown is white symbolizing purity or righteousness. this bride has been made in right standing with God.

She has been given a string of pain. You see a pearl is produced when a grain of sand pierces the shell of the oyster and it becomes an irritant to the oyster. That which is already inside the oyster will go to the irritant and begin releasing a fluid that brings healing. These fluids would have otherwise remained dormant had it not been for the irritant. Repeatedly, the irritant is covered and the pearl heals the wound. Those pearls are reminder that during the engagement life with him there will be irritations and trials that will be tailor made for the wearer. The pearls are reminder that he allows these things to come our way to build character and that during the irritations and trials; he is there to help us and to heal us.

She also has been given a veil and the veil is to be lifted only by the bridegroom. When he lifts the veil, he sees what no one else sees. She only has eyes for him. And when he looks at her he says, *"How beautiful you are, my darling! Oh, how beautiful! Your eyes behind your veil are doves. Your hair is like a flock of goats descending from the hills of Gilead. Your teeth are like a flock of sheep just shorn, coming up from the washing. Each has its twin; not one of them is alone. Your lips are like a scarlet ribbon; your mouth is lovely. Your temples behind your veil are like the halves of a pomegranate. You are altogether beautiful, my darling; there is no flaw in you." Song of Solomon 4: 1-4, 7* His bride is about to go through the process of preparation.

The Preparation

Husbands, love your wives, just as Christ loved the church and gave himself up for her to make her holy, cleansing her by the washing with water through the word, and to present her to himself as a radiant church, without stain or wrinkle or any other blemish, but holy and blameless. (Ephesians 5: 25-27)

He wants his bride to be perfect when he presents her to his father. He wants her to imitate him. He wants her to be transformed into his image. He wants her to be full of light instead of darkness. He wants her to be salt that has not lost its savor. He wants her to be overflowing with praise to him. He wants his bride to have a thankful heart and he wants her to be obedient and submissive to him.

We, his church, his bride is work in progress. We are awaiting the arrival of the bridegroom; Jesus Christ. It has been a long engagement but it will prove to be worth the wait!

Watch therefore for you know neither the day nor the hour in which the sound command is coming Matthew 25:13

He wants his bride packed and ready to go! The Lord is saying, "Where are you today? I have selected you. I have courted you and today I am proposing to you. Will you accept me?" To others he has selected you. he courted you, proposed to you and you have said yes to him and accepted him. And you are now in preparation. He is saying to you, "Today is the day to reaffirm your commitment to me."

LET'S GET CREATIVE

The bride of Christ is a theme that will allow you great creativity. Begin by sending out wedding invitations and the actual event will be a wedding reception. Any color combination will do. You do not have to go with the traditional wedding reception. You could use wedding memorabilia on each table as the centerpieces. You could possibly use wedding hats, gloves, veils wedding albums, hatboxes, strings of pearls etc. Each lady could be asked to bring in her own wedding picture and you could either use these as a separate display or include them as part of the centerpiece. You can have some of the ladies, who could still get into them, model their wedding gowns. You could also ask one of the local wedding boutiques to put on a fashion show for you. It would be great for all the brides to be and wonderful advertising for the boutique. You could have several women share, "the funniest thing happened at my wedding." As always, the goal is that women would except Christ as their personal savior and this would be a wonderful opportunity for the believers to make a recommitment. You can have the prayer of commitment on parchment paper rolled and tied with a white or red ribbon to symbolize the cleansing blood of Christ. And the prayer of recommitment on parchment paper, rolled and tied with a purple ribbon to symbolize the royal priesthood of the believer. You can have the scrolls as part of the centerpiece and at the appropriate time in the program they could choose. The food for this tea would be anything or everything you would have at a wedding reception.

PRAYER OF COMMITMENT
June 10, 2017

Father it is written in your word it if I confess with my mouth Jesus is Lord and believe in my heart that you have raised him from the dead I shall be saved. Father, I confess that I believe and I am asking you to forgive me of my sins. Jesus, please come into my heart and become Lord of my life. I renounce, at this very moment my past life of sin and I thank you for the new life that I have now received in Christ Jesus. Thank you for forgiving me of all my sin. Thank you that I am now a new creation. Now help me to love you and to really know you. Lord help me to live a life of obedience to you all the days of my life. I commit everything that I am or could ever hope to be to you. Amen

PRAYER OF RE-COMMITMENT
June 10, 2017

"Father, as a groom and his bride enter into covenant relationship, I affirm his day that I am in covenant relationship with you. Lord, I make a conscious, intelligent decision, this day, to make a vow of re-commitment to you. From this moment on:

I purpose to walk in your love, and in the light of your word.

I purpose to live a life of obedience to you, giving you priority in my life, allowing you to change in in whatever way you see fit.

I purpose to know you, to know your will and your ways and to allow you to love through me.

I purpose, from this moment forward to seek out what you have called me to do for your kingdom and to do the best I can in whatever you ask of me.

I acknowledge this day that you are the covenant keeping God. Amen

www.ingramcontent.com/pod-product-compliance
Lightning Source LLC
Chambersburg PA
CBHW031417040426
42444CB00005B/608